20th Century

Communications

Mark Lambert

Wayland

Titles in this series
Art
Cinema
Communications
Fashion
Farming
Medicine
Transport
Warfare

Editor: Francesca Motisi

Designer: Charles Harford HSD

Front cover, main picture An engineer adjusts one of the microwave dishes on London's Telecom Tower. Microwave links are often referred to as 'invisible highways in the sky'. They can carry thousands of telephone signals and television transmissions simultaneously.

Front cover, inset The switchboard at the Royal Exchange, Manchester, 1895.

Back cover One of the Intelsat 5 *satellites in geostationary orbit.*

First published in 1988 by
Wayland (Publishers) Ltd
61 Western Road, Hove
East Sussex BN3 1JD, England

© Copyright 1988 Wayland (Publishers) Ltd

British Library Cataloguing in Publication Data
Lambert, Mark, *1946–*
20th Century Communications.
1. Communication systems – For children
I. Title   II. Series
621.38

ISBN 1–85210–315–9

Typeset by Kalligraphics Ltd, Horley, Surrey, England
Printed by G.. Canale and C.S.p.A., Turin, Italy
Bound by Casterman, S.A., Belgium

Contents

Instant Communications

Below *The ancient Egyptians used a form of picture writing known as heiroglyphics.*

The invention of the electric telegraph in the middle of the nineteenth century changed the world, as rapid communications suddenly became possible. But by the turn of the century, telephone and radio communications were starting to make an even greater impact.

In the modern world, the term 'communications' is often used when describing very complicated systems, like 'telecommunications' and 'communications satellites'. But communication is, in fact, very simple; it is just the process of conveying information or ideas from one person to another. In order to communicate effectively, early humans evolved speech and developed languages. Alphabets developed from picture-writing and the invention of the printing press in the mid-1400s enabled people to communicate printed words to huge numbers of people.

Below *In 1438 Johann Gutenberg devised a printing press that used movable metal type It thus became possible to print a number of copies of the same work.*

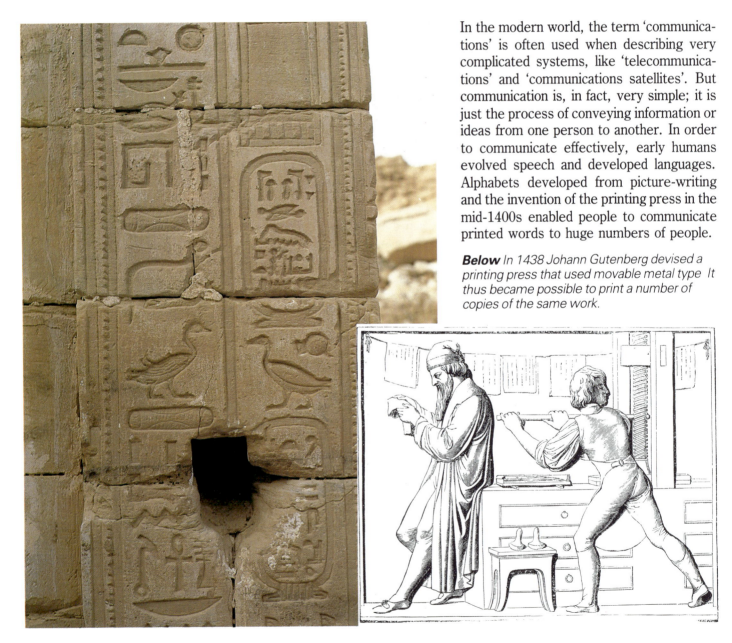

For many centuries, however, communicating over long distances remained a slow process. Messengers travelled on foot, on horseback or in ships, and a message could take many months to reach its destination. Sometimes visual signals, such as bonfires or flashes of sunlight produced by a mirror, could be used. And in 1793 Claude Chappe, a French clergyman, devised what he called the semaphore telegraph. This had a pair of movable arms mounted on a tower and different positions of the arms indicated different letters, words or phrases. Long lines of such towers were used to send messages from one place to another.

Of course, visual signals required the sender and receiver of the signal to be able to see each other. A foggy day could therefore make communications impossible. Even on fine days a message could still take quite a long time to travel any distance. On the other hand, electricity travels almost instantly down a wire, so the invention of the electric telegraph heralded the beginning of instant communications.

The electric telegraph

The electric telegraph was first proposed by an unknown Scotsman in 1753. During the next ninety years several inventors built telegraph systems, all of which used a number of separate wires to indicate the different letters of the alphabet. The last of these was the five-wire system built in 1837 by the British inventors William Cooke and Charles Wheatstone. Electric current passing along the wires caused magnetic needles to point to letters on a diagram. However, in 1838, the American inventor Samuel Morse devised his code of dots and dashes, which could be transmitted down a wire.

Left Sailors aboard the Great Eastern *prepare to grapple for a lost cable during an attempt to lay a transatlantic telegraph cable in 1865. During the following year a cable was successfully laid.*

The first working telegraph line linked Baltimore and Washington DC and by the 1850s there were telegraph networks throughout North America and Europe. Messages were only slowed down by the fact that operators had to code and decode messages by hand. In 1855, Professor David Hughes, a British scientist, invented a printing telegraph that turned letters into electrical signals automatically. At the receiving end another machine decoded the signals and printed out the message. The first successful transatlantic telegraph cable was laid by Isambard Kingdom Brunel's huge steamship, the *Great Eastern*, in 1866. By 1900 it was possible for people to go to their nearest telegraph office and send a message in Morse Code almost anywhere in Europe or North America. The first telegraph subscriber service was introduced in Berlin in 1903. About 100 companies had their own equipment and operators could send messages to other subscribers via an exchange.

Pictures as well as words could be transmitted – by the process known as facsimile transmission. Often thought of as a modern invention, this was actually invented by a German scientist called Arthur Korn in 1902 and first used in 1907. It was done by using a photoelectric cell to detect the light and dark areas of a picture which was placed on a rotating drum.

The invention of the telephone

The telegraph transmits only coded signals. In 1875, however, the American inventor Alexander Graham Bell was working on a device intended to transmit several telegraph messages simultaneously. By chance he discovered that a vibrating reed, producing several different notes at the same time, could be made to generate sufficient current to make another reed at the end of a wire reproduce the same notes. In 1876 he succeeded in transmitting recognizable words and he patented his telephone in March of that year, just beating another American inventor, Elisha Gray. In the following year, the prolific American inventor Thomas Alva Edison produced a telephone with a separate mouthpiece – Bell's single, combined microphone and earpiece was difficult to use.

The first telephone exchange opened in January 1878, at New Haven, Connecticut in the USA. It had eight lines, each of which served two or three customers. The first telephone exchange in Britain opened in 1879. By the 1880s there were many small local exchanges in both the USA and Europe and the Bell telephone company introduced the first long-distance telephone line in 1884, between Boston and New York. At this time all calls had to be connected by an operator. But in 1889 Almon Strowger, an undertaker in Kansas City, believing that this system was losing him business, devised an automatic telephone exchange. His system allowed callers to obtain local numbers by processing a combination of three buttons, which were soon replaced by a rotary dial.

Right In 1878 Thomas Edison improved Bell's telephone by separating the microphone and earpiece, thus making talking and listening easier.

However, this system was only adopted by small, local telephone companies. Long distance calls still had to be connected by the operator. In 1900 an American physicist, Michael Pupin, patented an induction coil that greatly increased the efficiency of long telephone lines. A number of such coils, placed at 1 km intervals along the line, made it possible for people to talk to each other over long distances.

Communication without wires

The telegraph, telephone and gramophone made important contributions to the progress of communications. But it was the development of radio that made the greatest impact. The existence of radio waves had originally been suggested by the Scottish scientist James Maxwell in the 1860s. His ideas were proved right in 1887 by a German scientist, Heinrich Hertz, who used a simple transmitter to make sparks jump between two knobs in a receiver. Hertz's apparatus could transmit only over very short distances. But other scientists were soon experimenting with more powerful transmitters and more sensitive receivers. The Italian engineer Guglielmo Marconi achieved the greatest success. During the 1890s he sent signals over increasing distances and in 1900 he devised the tuned circuit, which enables a receiver to be tuned to a particular wavelength. In 1901 he succeeded in transmitting a signal across the Atlantic from Cornwall in Britain to Newfoundland in Canada.

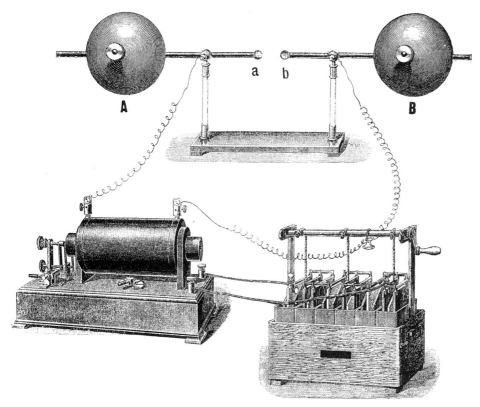

Left Hertz's transmitter. Current from a battery (bottom right) was discharged into an induction coil (bottom left), a device for increasing the voltage.

Below Guglielmo Marconi and two assistants at Signal Hill, St John's, Newfoundland in December 1901, when the first transatlantic radio signal was received from a transmitter at Poldhu in Cornwall, Britain. This was a tremendous achievement, but exactly how the signal had managed to travel this distance despite the curvature of the Earth remained a mystery for 23 years (see page 17).

Right *Marconi in the wireless room of his yacht* Electra *(1920).*

Below *When the murderer Dr Harvey Crippen and Ethel Le Neve (posing as his 'son') sailed from Britain on the SS* Montrose, *they imagined that they were safe from pursuit. But a radio message was sent notifying the Captain that the fugitives were on board and they were arrested. News of their arrest was radioed to Canada and relayed back to Britain by telegraph. Newspapers carried the story within days of the arrest.*

Marconi radios were soon being installed on ships, and by 1903 the British Admiralty could keep in touch with eighty Royal Navy ships. In 1910, the murderer Harvey Crippen was arrested on board the SS *Montrose* as a result of a radio message. And in 1912 radio helped save the lives of many on board the supposedly unsinkable British liner the *Titanic*, after she struck an iceberg.

During the First World War radio played an important part in several naval battles and in aircraft communications.

Meanwhile, other important inventions were being developed. Early radio receivers used a device called a coherer to detect radio waves. In 1906 it was discovered that crystals of some materials were much better at detecting radio waves. But soon crystals were replaced by the diode valve, devised in 1904 by the English scientist John Ambrose Fleming. The triode valve, invented in 1906 by the American engineer Lee de Forest, could be used to amplify radio signals, which could then be fed to a loudspeaker. In 1906, Reginald Fessenden, an American scientist living in Massachusetts, built a transmitter that could send speech. He broadcast a Christmas programme that was heard by many radio-operators on nearby ships. In 1915 the first voice was transmitted across the Atlantic. The American Telephone and Telegraph Company (AT&T) sent a message that was received by a radio station on the Eiffel Tower in Paris.

By now a number of scientists were starting to believe in the possibility of transmitting pictures. In 1884, a German inventor, Paul Nipkow, had invented an ingenious disc. When this was spun, a spiral of holes passed light from a scene to a light-sensitive, photoelectric cell. This information could be transmitted by radio signal and by reversing the process at the receiver, a picture of the scene could be created on a screen. Then, in 1897, a device called the cathode ray tube (the basis of the modern television tube) was invented by a German scientist, Ferdinand Braun. In 1906 a Russian scientist, Professor Boris Rosing, devised the first very crude working television system, using a Nipkow disc to create the signal and a cathode ray tube to display the picture. In 1908, Campbell Swinton, a Scottish engineer, published a proposal for a completely electronic television system. He suggested that the cathode ray tube could not only be used as a receiver but could also be modified for use as a camera. Fifteen years later his ideas were proved right.

Left *The Cunard liner* Carpathia *picking up survivors from the White Star Line's* Titanic. *At ten minutes after midnight on 15 April 1912 the* Carpathia *had received the radio signal C.Q.D. (Come Quick, Danger), followed by the new alarm call S.O.S.*

Below *A Berliner gramophone.*

Recording sound

The recording of information is often an essential part of communications. In 1877 Thomas Edison was the first person to record sound that could be played back, and in the following year he began to market his phonograph. Sound vibrations were recorded by a needle vibrating up and down on a piece of tinfoil attached to a rotating drum. In 1886, Chichester Bell, a cousin of Alexander Graham Bell, devised an improved type phonograph known as the graphophone, which used wax cylinders instead of tinfoil. Two years later, in the USA, Emile Berliner, produced the first gramophone. His machine recorded a pattern of wavy lines in a layer of lamp black and linseed oil on a flat glass disc.

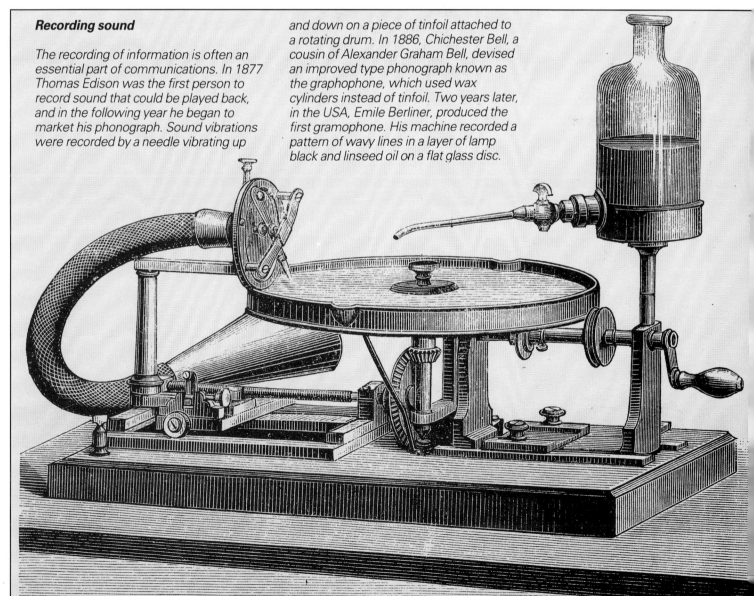

1918–1929

The Post-War Years

Telephone networks began to spread rapidly during the 1920s. At the same time, radio communications were greatly improved and television developed from an idea into reality.

Below Automatic telephone exchanges like this, which were introduced in Britain's major cities during the early 1920s, were in operation for many years. Such exchanges required fewer operators.

After the First World War, telephones began to be seen as a social necessity, rather than just a luxury and as an aid to businesses. By 1918 many of the smaller telephone companies in the USA had introduced automatic exchanges. But the largest company of all, the Bell Telephone Company, waited until 1919 before deciding that such exchanges were reliable. In Britain, Epsom got the first automatic exchange in 1912 and many small and medium-sized towns were soon equipped with Strowger exchanges, but they proved difficult to use in large cities. During the 1920s, the Automatic Telephone Manufacturing Company of Liverpool developed a piece of equipment called a director, which enabled a Strowger exchange to handle large

numbers of telephone calls. The first director exchange opened in Holborn, London in 1927. In the same year the first transatlantic telephone service was inaugurated. It used a radio link and could carry only one call at a time at a cost of £15!

Strowger exchanges were not the only type available. Another much faster type of automatic exchange, known as crossbar because of the shape of its switches, had been thought of in 1901. The first patent was taken out by the Bell Telephone Company in 1915 and later work was mostly carried out in Sweden, where the first crossbar exchange was installed in 1926. However, more than ten years passed before crossbar exchanges were used anywhere else.

A candlestick telephone of 1924. The first telephones did not have dials but in the 1920s when automatic exchanges were introduced dials became necessary. When a number was dialled electrical impulses were sent to the exchange which operated special switches which connected you with the telephone number you wanted.

Above In the early 1920s people could listen
to regular broadcasts on crystal radio sets.

Radio

During the First World War, Guglielmo Marconi, while in charge of Italy's radio service, pioneered the method of flying blind in an aeroplane by following a radio beam. After the war he did a great deal of work on short wave and VHF (Very High Frequency) transmission and by the mid-1920s short waves were being used to transmit messages over long distances – to the USA and even to Australia. Radio waves travel in straight lines and until this time the way in which transmissions overcame the curvature of the Earth had seemed somewhat mysterious. But in 1924 the British physicist Edward Appleton showed that radio waves are reflected off a layer in the atmosphere called the ionosphere. The Earth's surface also reflects radio waves, which can therefore travel round the world by bouncing up and down between the ground (or sea) and the ionosphere.

Regular broadcasts, aimed at informing and entertaining people began during the 1920s. To begin with people listened on simple crystal sets that needed no source of power. But soon the superheterodyne receiver, or superhet, invented in 1918 by Major Edwin Armstrong of the US army, was being widely used. Armstrong's invention made it much easier to tune into radio stations and pick up weak signals.

Below (top) The first superheterodyne radio receiver, invented in 1918, was still being used by the US Signal Corps in 1926.

Below By 1922 a family in Britain could listen to music broadcast from Holland.

Above In 1926, John Logie Baird demonstrated his television system in London. Pictures of Baird holding 'Stukey Bill' and another ventroloquist doll were transmitted to a receiving station.

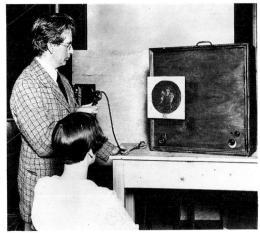

Right Baird at the receiver, looking at a picture of an assistant holding the dolls.

The first television

During the 1920s inventors in a number of countries, notably the USA, Britain, and the USSR, were trying to develop working television systems. One such inventor was Vladimir Zworykin, who had been taught as a student by Boris Rosing at St Petersburg (now Leningrad) in the USSR. In 1919, Zworykin went to America, where he joined the Westinghouse Company, and in 1923 he began developing a fully electronic camera tube, which he called the iconoscope.

Zworykin's first system was crude; it could transmit nothing more than a shape projected on to the camera tube. It took eight years to develop this into a practical working system. Meanwhile, the Scottish inventor John Logie Baird, was having more success with a mechanical system, based on the use of Nipkow discs. In 1925 Baird transmitted the first live picture of a human and in the following year he demonstrated his television to members of the Royal Institution in London. In 1928 he succeeded in transmitting three people's faces from London to New York. To gain further publicity, he then demonstrated several of his inventions, including stereoscopic television and the first colour television – achieved by using a Nipkow disc equipped with green, red and blue filters. In 1929, Baird opened the first

experimental television studio in London. Baird and Zworykin had plenty of competitors. Other inventors included the Hungarian D. Von Mihaly, who devised a mechanical system that used mirrors on a rotating drum instead of the holes in the Nipkow disc. Baird eventually adopted this system himself. The Russian scientist Boris Grabovsky claimed to have made the first broadcast using an electronic system in 1926. And in the USA Charles Jenkins was carrying out experiments that were very similar to Baird's work in London. In 1927 AT&T used a mechanical system to broadcast a speech by Secretary of Commerce Herbert Hoover (who later became US President). By the end of 1928 there were eighteen experimental television stations in the USA, all broadcasting regular programmes.

Below John Logie Baird with an early version of his television system in 1925. The key to the system was the spinning Nipkow disc.

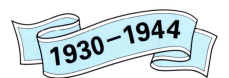

Dawn of the Television Age

The modern telegraph systems, Telex and TWX, were introduced during the 1930s. Soon afterwards, television became a practical reality.

Below *Receiving a telegram at the London Central Telegraph Office in 1934. The machine is of the type invented by Professor David Hughes in 1855.*

By 1930 the telegraph had largely been superseded by the telephone. But it gained a new lease of life in the 1930s, when telephone companies introduced teletypewriter exchange services. Each subscriber could now send printed messages direct to other subscribers via telephone lines. The American system, TWX, was introduced in 1931 and the British Telex system began in 1932. Both are still in use, although in the future they are likely to be replaced by computerized systems.

The number of telephone subscribers continued to increase during the 1930s, with the result that more and larger telephone exchanges had to be built. In Britain in 1932 it became possible to make a long-distance, or trunk, call without having to book it an hour or more in advance. Some familiar services were introduced during this period. The Speaking Clock was introduced in 1936 and the 999 Emergency Service began in 1937. In the USA an improved version of the crossbar exchange was introduced in 1940. Each selector could now carry up to ten calls instead of only one.

Left In Britain, the first Speaking Clock was compiled using the recorded voice of Miss Jane Cain.

Below The transmitter room of one of the chain of radar stations built along the south coast of Britain just before the Second World War.

Radar

As Europe prepared for war in the 1930s, another use for radio waves was also being investigated. In 1922 Marconi had suggested that it might be possible to detect ships by bouncing radio waves off them and in 1931 the first experiments on radar (radio direction and ranging) were carried out in Britain. During a test in 1935 pulses from a BBC transmitter at Daventry detected a bomber flying twelve kilometres away. By the outbreak of war in 1939, Britain had a chain of radar stations along the south coast. During the war, radar was used to great effect in ships and in aircraft.

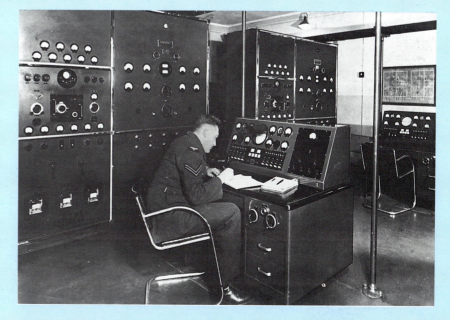

Electronic television

The 1930s also saw a rapid development in television. In 1929 John Logie Baird was already transmitting programmes, via a single transmitter supplied, reluctantly, by the British Broadcasting Corporation (BBC). In 1930 he was given another transmitter, which allowed him to transmit both pictures and sound at the same time. Meanwhile, however, others were developing electronic systems. In 1930, Philo T. Farnsworth, a young American inventor, patented an electronic television. In 1931, Vladimir Zworykin, now working for the Radio Corporation of America (RCA) perfected his electronic camera, or iconoscope. In 1934, Isaac Schoenburg and a team of researchers at Electrical and Musical Industries (EMI) developed their own electronic camera, known as the Emitron, and in the same year teamed up with the Marconi company to develop a fully electronic television system.

The world's first television service was inaugurated in Germany in 1935. It used mechanical cameras, which were used to scan film for broadcasting. The pictures were low definition, consisting of just 180 lines. In 1936, the BBC started the first live, high definition public television service,

Opposite A Marconi-EMI Emitron television camera outside Alexandra Palace in London in 1936.

Left In 1935 Baird Television Ltd, based at Crystal Palace in London, demonstrated a high definition television system known as Intermediate Film Technique. The scene was filmed using an ordinary film camera. The film was passed directly to a developing tank and the wet negative film was then scanned by the television camera, about a minute after the original filming. Using this technique Baird showed pictures of horses jumping, men boxing and extracts from films.

Stereo recording

Stereophonic recording was invented in Britain at EMI in the early 1930s. The system they used was basically the same as the one used today – two microphones record separate tracks on each side of the groove on the disc. However, stereophonic records were not sold to the public for another twenty–five years.

broadcasting from Alexandra Palace in North London. To begin with, Baird's electro-mechanical system and Marconi-EMI's electronic system were both used. But although Baird had raised the definition from thirty to 240 lines he made a number of other improvements, the mechanical system proved to be fraught with difficulties. The Marconi-EMI system, on the other hand, could produce 405 line pictures. It was also reliable and easy to use. Within a few months the superiority of the electronic system became obvious and Baird's television was abandoned forever.

By the late 1930s there were television services in a number of other countries, including Germany, the USSR and France. Television cameras were present at several notable events and occasions, including the 1936 Berlin Olympic Games, the coronation of George VI in 1937 and the *Tour de France* in 1938. In the USA the first fully electronic television service was introduced by RCA in 1939. One year later colour television was introduced by Peter Goldmark of the Columbia Broadcasting System (CBS). The camera had a disc of three coloured filters that rotated in front of the tube. The receiver had a similar, much larger disc that rotated in front of the screen in time with the camera disc.

Television broadcasts ceased in Britain and the USSR during the Second World War and by 1942 there were few programmes being shown in the USA. In France the television service was taken over by the Germans in 1940. German television continued until the Berlin transmitter was hit by a bomb in 1943.

Below Right *The television pictures demonstrated by Baird in 1935 could be received in the home using a Baird Cathode Ray television receiver.*

Below *The control room at the Marconi-EMI television station at Alexandra Palace in 1936.*

Left Testing the cameras and other equipment that were about to be used to televise the coronation of George VI in 1937.

Above The Ecko-Scophony television receiver was revealed at the Radiolympia exhibition of 1936. It cost 100 guineas.

The Transistor Age

After the Second World War, developments in communications included electronic colour television and a transatlantic telephone cable. But the most important event was the invention of the transistor.

Below An early radio receiver, showing the glass diode valve.

Without the invention of the diode and triode valves in the early 1900s, progress in electronic communication would have been impossible; there would have been no radio and no television. Valves were also important in the construction of the new electronic computers, which started to appear in the 1940s. But valves were bulky and unreliable.

ENIAC (Electronic Numerical Integrator And Calculator), the electronic computer built in 1946 at the University of Pennsylvania in the USA, contained 18,000 triode valves and took up over 760 cubic metres of space. The valves consumed as much power (and generated as much heat) as 150 1 kilowatt electric fires and every few minutes at least one valve would burn out.

In 1947 William Shockley, John Bardeen and Walter Brattain, working at the Bell Laboratories in the USA, invented a new kind of electronic device, the transistor. Like the valve, this could be used to amplify an electric current or as an electronic switch. But the transistor was much smaller than the valve, consumed a fraction of the power and did not have to warm up before starting to work. During the next few years transistors were made even smaller, more robust and more reliable. By 1956 production of transistors had risen to over 25,000 a year.

Above An early portable radio in 1947. It weighed just over 2 kilograms and contained four battery powered diode valves.

Colour television and transistor radios

Colour television pictures were first transmitted in the USA, using the spinning disc system invented by Peter Goldmark in 1940. However, the experiment was not a success. The new, expensive colour sets could not receive the normal black and white transmissions, and existing black and white sets could not receive the colour transmissions, even in black and white.

In 1953, however, the first fully electronic system of colour television was a complete success. It was originally developed in 1949 by a team of scientists at RCA in the USA and was basically the same system that is still used today. Instead of a single beam of electrons, as in a black and white television, there are three beams, each carrying a different colour signal. These pass through a shadow mask and cause red, green or blue phosphor dots to glow on the screen.

Left By 1949 truly portable 'handbag' radios were becoming popular. This model contained four diode valves.

Tape recorders

In 1932, the BBC recorded King George V's Christmas speech on a machine known as Blattnerphone. This used steel tape to record the magnetic pattern of sound. In 1935 the first plastic recording tape, coated with iron oxide, was produced by two German companies, AEG Telefunken and I.G. Farben. In the years just before and during the Second World War, German radio stations used tape recorders, enabling programme controllers to edit out any mistakes before items were transmitted. They could also repeat programmes more than once.

Left This picture shows making a tape recording for broadcast to Australia from London in 1954.

Left *Long-playing records appeared in the late 1940s. This 'automat' is really a woman hidden in a room who watches a control board, and from light indicators, selects the chosen record from a central file.*

Transistors did not replace valves in televisions until the 1960s. But the first transistor radio was developed in 1954 by an American Company called Regency. The Japanese company Sony introduced a transistor radio in 1955 and within a few years bulky valve radios were a thing of the past. At about the same time transistors were replacing valves in mainframe computers, which were therefore also becoming much smaller.

In the late 1940s, plastics began to replace shellac for making records. As a result the grooves could be made smaller and closer together and long-playing records started to be made. Magnetic tape for recording stored computer information was introduced during the 1950s and the music industry began to use tapes to make master recordings before manufacturing records. At the same time reel-to-reel tape recorders became generally available to the public. Recording television video signals on tape was more difficult, because they contain so much information. In 1956 the Ampex company of California, USA, succeeded in recording a television signal on a 5 cm wide magnetic tape running at 37.5 cm a second. In the same year the first telephone cable was laid across the Atlantic between Scotland and Newfoundland.

1957-1975

The Space Age

The invention of the silicon chip made it possible to achieve a huge reduction in the size of electronic equipment — much greater than that produced by the transistor. The new technology led to the development of such things as electronic telephone exchanges, hi-fi systems and video recorders. At the same time the development of satellites made instant world-wide communications a reality.

Below A single silicon chip may contain hundreds or thousands of electronic components.

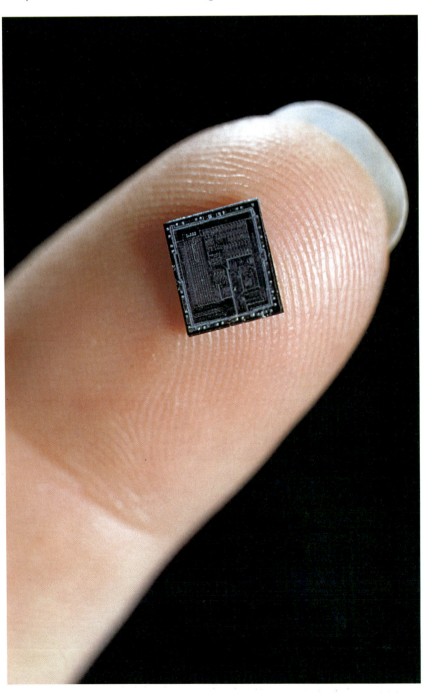

Future historians may regard the silicon chip as the world's most influential twentieth-century invention. Known originally as the integrated circuit, it was devised in 1958 by scientists at Texas Instruments in the USA. Their invention made it possible to form several different electronic components (transistors, resistors, diodes, capacitors and others), together with their interconnections, on a single, tiny slice of silicon. During the next few years scientists succeeded in placing tens, hundreds and finally thousands of components on to silicon chips. The single-chip microprocessor, containing all the components of a computer central processor, was devised by Edward Hoof of the American Intel Corporation and patented in 1971. By the early 1970s minicomputers were being linked together to form networks, making it possible to transfer information from place to place at very high speed. The first microcomputer, the Altair 8800, was built by Ed Roberts of Micro Intrumentation and Telemetry Systems (MITS) in 1974.

Satellite communications

Meanwhile, the space age was in full swing. In addition to the hundreds of space probes, manned spacecraft and observation satellites that had been launched over the years, there were also a number of communications satellites, whose purpose was simply to improve communications here on Earth. In 1960, the American satellite *Echo 1* was launched. Once in orbit 1600 km above the

Earth's surface, it was inflated and became a huge balloon over 30 m across. It was then used as a simple reflector, to bounce back radio signals aimed at it from the ground. However, the returning signals were not boosted or amplified in any way and were therefore rather weak. Later the same year, the US army launched *Courier 1B*, the first communications satellite with its own amplifiers. Power was supplied by over 19,000 solar cells (invented by the Bell Telephone Company in 1954) and the whole satellite weighed about 250 kg. Unfortunately, it worked for only eighteen days.

Above Telstar, *launched in July 1962 was the first public communications satellite.*

In July 1962 the American National Aeronautics and Space Administration (NASA) launched *Telstar*, the first public communications satellite. Built and operated by AT&T, it was powered by 3,600 solar cells and weighed just 77 kg. Within hours of its launch *Telstar* helped to transmit the first live television pictures across the Atlantic. It could also carry up to sixty telephone conversations. In 1963 the satellite *Relay 1* transmitted the first colour television pictures.

The orbit of *Telstar* was relatively low, and ground stations could only maintain contact with it for twenty minutes at a time. The solution to this problem was to place a satellite in a high, geostationary orbit, so that it would remain 35,880 km above the same spot on the Earth's Equator all the time. Just three geostationary satellites would be required to relay signals to and from any point on the Earth. In 1965 the American communications satellite *Early Bird* was launched into a geostationary orbit and on 28 June it became the first commercial satellite to provide a constant link between America and Europe. It was later renamed *Intelsat 1* and in 1966 three *Intelsat 2* satellites began providing a world-wide communications link. The most modern satellites, the *Instelsat 5* series, can carry two television channels and up to 12,000 telephone conversations. During the 1970s Canada and America both launched their own internal satellite communications systems.

Below *The communications satellite* Intelsat 5.

Electronics and telephones

In the late 1950s it became clear that the new electronic devices that were starting to appear might be very useful in telephone systems. Engineers quickly realized that electronic exchanges would be smaller, faster, more reliable and cheaper to operate. The first trials were carried out in 1960 by the Bell Telephone Company at Illinois in the USA. In 1966, the Post Office in Britain opened the first TXE2 electronic exchange, with a capacity of 7,000 lines. This type of exchange is controlled electronically, but

uses a type of mechanical switch called a reed relay rather than electronic switches. The TXE2 exchange and the larger TXE4 version proved to be a success and the manufacture of Strowger exchanges began to be phased out. Some crossbar exchanges were installed in Britain until TXE2 exchanges became available in sufficient numbers in the late 1960s. Also in 1966 work began on the development of optical fibres to replace the now outdated copper cables (see page 45).

Above *Signals from satellites are received by ground based stations. This station is in Muscat.*

Space communications

The first satellite was launched by the Soviets on 4 October 1957, called Sputnik 1. One month later Sputnik 2 sent back information about the condition of its passenger, the dog Laika. In February 1958 America's satellite Explorer 1 sent back signals that led to the discovery of the Van Allen radiation belts that surround the Earth. And in December 1958 the US launched a satellite named SCORE that broadcast a number of prerecorded messages to the people of America. The first pictures of the Moon were transmitted back to Earth by the Soviet probe Luna 3 in October 1959. In 1966 Luna 9 sent the first television pictures from the Moon's surface and in 1969 the world watched the first manned Moon landing on television. At the same time the first unmanned space probes were starting to investigate Venus, and during the 1970s and 1980s people were able to see remarkable pictures of Mars, Jupiter, Saturn, and Uranus sent back by the Viking, Pioneer and Voyager spacecraft.

Since the 1960s a variety of different types of observation satellite have been launched into orbit around the Earth. Among these are weather satellites, earth resources satellites, military ('spy') satellites and astronomical satellites.

Right Launched in September 1977 Voyager 1 flew past Jupiter in March 1979 and Saturn in November 1980.

Television and recording

The first all-transistor television was produced by the Japanese company Sony in 1960, at which time it became possible to manufacture truly portable televisions. In 1973 it became possible to link computers to the televisions in people's homes, when television companies introduced teletext, the first videotex system. Anyone with a specially adapted television could now call up stored information and display it on the screen, simply by pressing buttons on a key-pad.

Meanwhile, hi-fi systems had appeared. These used the latest electronic technology for playing and recording music. Portable tape recorders appeared after the first tape cassettes were introduced in the 1960s. The first video tape cassettes were produced in 1969 by Sony, who produced Betamax video recorders for use in the home in 1975.

Opposite *US President John Kennedy, his wife Jackie and Vice President Lyndon Johnson watch America's first manned space flight on a portable television in 1961.*

Left *A modern video camera, video recorder and recording tapes.*

Below *A transistor radio of the late 1960s.*

The Computer Age

The development of ever smaller and more powerful computer systems has helped to create a revolution in communications. Today, information can not only be transmitted instantly, but processed almost instantly as well.

Modern communications form part of what has become known as information technology (IT). This is technology based on the microprocessor silicon chip, using a mix of telecommunications, television and office automation techniques and is concerned with the instant processing of speech, text and visual information as well as its instant transmission. Microprocessors can now be found in cars, televisions, telephones and washing machines. Communications systems are now beginning to rely more and more on the use of computers and the transmission of digital signals.

Below *Modern merchant banking relies heavily on the use of computer technology.*

Computer communications

In 1979 the British Post Office launched the world's first public viewdata system now known as Prestel. At the same time microcomputers were starting to play an increasingly important part in communications. Desktop personal computers, complete with monitors and keyboards, first appeared in 1977, and today a microcomputer can be used to send messages to other computer users, a process known as electronic mail. All that is required is a device called a modem, which connects the computer into the telephone system, and appropriate piece of software (computer program) and, usually, a subscription to the company providing the communications service. In Britain, computer communications services include Prestel, Telecom Gold and One-to-

One, all of which provide electronic mail, telex, notice-board, database and radio-paging services. It is also possible to contact a number of private bulletin boards.

In the future computer communications will probably be used more and more for such things as banking and shopping. Banks already use their own computer systems for keeping track of customers' accounts. Eventually, everyone will be able to use their home computers to do such things as paying bills and transferring money from one account to another. Major stores already use computers for stock control, price checking, and so on. Soon it will be possible to present a magnetized plastic card at a computer terminal in a shop and have your own account automatically debited with the right amount. And eventually it should be possible to order a variety of goods from home using your own personal computer.

Television, recording and radio

Miniaturization of electronic circuits has made it possible to produce smaller and smaller televisions. The first flat-screen pocket television appeared in 1980 and the first wristwatch television was produced in 1983. They use liquid crystal displays instead of the standard television tube and, in fact, until recently this type of display has only been suitable for very small screens. Soon, however, scientists hope to produce a full-size flat screen television that can hang on a wall like a picture.

Meanwhile satellite television has been developed and many television stations now beam their programmes at satellites. Such signals may be picked up by receiving stations and retransmitted to viewers, but with the right satellite receiving dish, it is now possible to receive pictures directly from satellites.

Cable television is another recent development. The viewer's television is linked to the broadcasting company directly by a cable, which may carry many different channels. This system makes it possible to have interactive television, in which viewers can respond to programmes, be polled on issues, cast votes or even question people being interviewed.

Opposite A wide range of audio and video equipment is now available. Shown here are two stereo radio/cassette players, a personal stereo cassette player and a miniature television.

Below Inside the studio of a cable television broadcasting company.

Above A pocket-sized personal stereo radio.

Opposite A large but portable stereo radio-cassette player.

Right Modern audio systems can be built up using tuners, single or twintape players, compact disc players, record turntables and speakers.

In the future, digital television will make it possible for sets to convert signals into pictures with virtually perfect quality. At the same time the viewer will be able to control the screen to produce a variety of different effects. It will be possible to show two different channels on a split screen, zoom in on part of a picture, as well as producing slow motion and freeze frame.

Some of these effects can already be produced using a modern video recorder, of which the most popular type is now the Video Home System (VHS), introduced by Sony in the early 1980s. Video discs were also introduced in the 1980s, but the high quality sound produced by compact audio discs have made them even more popular. Video discs can also be used to store huge amounts of computer information, including such things as film sequences and maps. This system makes it possible to have interactive video, in which the viewer chooses what happens by controlling the order in which the video frames are played.

Most microcomputers now use magnetic disks – floppy disks or hard disks – rather than tape. But among the latest development in audio technology is digital audio tape, which may soon rival the compact disc for quality. Among the most popular innovations in audio technology are the personal stereo radio/cassette players and the larger portable stereo systems.

Right A portable phone uses the cellular radio system to allow the user to make and receive calls anywhere inside the area covered by the system.

Below Examining a circuit board at one of British Telecom's System X electronic telephone exchanges.

Telegraph and telephone

In spite of the ease of using the telephone, the telegraph still remains popular for business use. Telex messages and facsimile copies of pictures and documents can be sent to almost anywhere in the developed world. During the 1980s several countries have introduced teletex, a high speed form of telex designed to link word processors. Unlike public telex, which only has enough codes to print capital letters, teletex can use both upper and lower-case letters.

Telephone systems are starting to rely more and more on electronic devices. Already, many homes have push-button electronic telephones and there are now many digital telephone exchanges in service. In Britain, British Telecom hope to have a completely digital system, based on the new System X electronic exchanges, in operation

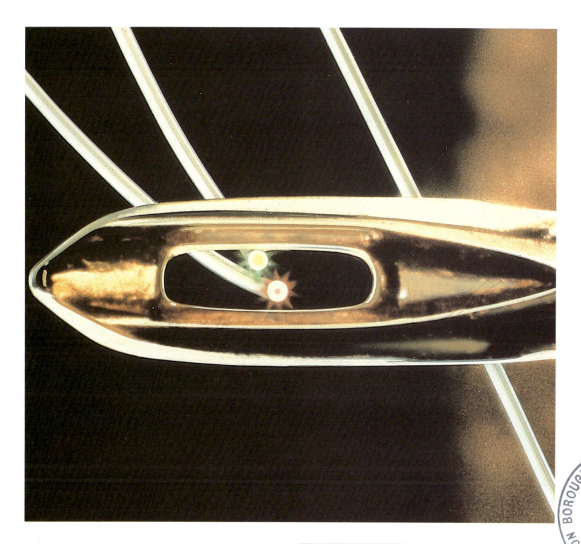

Left *Optical fibres, so fine that several can be threaded through the eye of a needle, are now being used to carry communication signals. An optical fibre is a thin, glass fibre, specially made so that light entering at one end travels to the other. The sides of the fibre reflect the light inwards, so that none escapes. The signal being transmitted is used to control a light source, such as a light-emitting diode or a laser, and the light from this is fed into the fibre. Cables containing optical fibres can be made much thinner and lighter than copper cables. And an optical fibre can carry many more signals than a copper wire – a single pair of optical fibres can carry over 1,900 telephone conversations.*

by the year 2000. At the same time optical fibres are being used to replace many copper cables, and light rather than electricity is being used to transmit signals. Eventually a single optical fibre to each home could provide a variety of communications services, including cable television, computer shopping, home banking and the telephone.

Another telephone service that is becoming increasingly popular is the mobile phone, or cellular radio phone, which allows a subscriber to make or receive a call anywhere within a reception area of the system. Video-conferencing uses both television and telephone links and allows groups of business people in different parts of the world to see one another as they talk. Some people believe that we may all eventually have videophones (viewphones). However, such a system is likely to remain very expensive and it is quite possible that people will never actually want it.

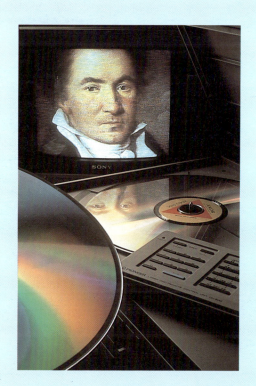

Laser discs

A laser disc contains information in the form of a spiral of microscopic pits. A laser beam is used to etch the pits into a master disc, which is then used to make copies. In the finished copies the pits are formed in a layer of highly reflective material and can thus be 'read' by another laser on the disc player. They are covered in a protective layer and, because nothing actually touches the disc when it is played, it will last almost indefinitely.

Glossary

Amplifier   An electronic device, such as a transistor or triode valve, that increases the strength of an electrical signal.

AT&T   American Telegraph & Telephone Company.

BBC   British Broadcasting Corporation.

Cathode ray tube   An electronic device in which a beam of electrons (cathode rays) are made to strike a fluorescent screen, which glows as a result.

Compact disc   A laser disc used for reproducing music and speech.

Diode valve   A type of thermionic valve that contains just two electrodes. Because it passes electrical current in one direction only, it can be used as a rectifier to produce direct current from alternating current. A diode can also be made of a semiconductor material and is an essential component of a tuning circuit for detecting radio signals.

Electric current   The flow of 'free' electrons through a conductor.

Electromagnet   A temporary magnet formed by winding a coil of wire around a piece of iron. Electrical current flowing in the wire causes the iron to become magnetized and a varying electrical current produces a corresponding variation in the magnetic field.

Electromagnetic radiation   An invisible, wave-like emission, composed of vibrating electrical and magnetic fields, that travels at the speed of light. Such emissions form the range known as the electromagnetic spectrum, which includes cosmic rays, X-rays, ultra-voilet rays, light, infra-red rays, microwaves and radio waves.

Electronic   Concerned with the accurately controlled flow of electrons through a vacuum, gas or semiconductor.

Electrons   The minute, negatively-charged particles that move around the nucleus of an atom.

EMI   Electrical and Musical Industries.

Hi-fi system   A combination of a record turntable, one or more tape players, tuners, amplifiers and loudspeakers designed to produce high quality (High Fidelity) reproduction of music and speech.

Laser   A device for producing an intense, uniform beam of light of a single colour, or wavelength.

Light-emitting diode   A type of diode that glows like a tiny bulb when electric current passes through it.

Magnetic field   The region around a magnet or a current-carrying wire in which a magnetic force exerts an influence.

Magnetic tape   Plastic tape coated with iron oxide and other materials. The iron atoms can be magnetized and a varying magnetic field produces a pattern of magnetization on the tape.

Photoelectric cell   A device in which light energy is converted into electricity energy.

Radio   The use of electromagnetic radiation to transmit electrical signals without wires.

RCA   Radio Corporation of America.

Semiconductor   A material that can, under different circumstances, behave as a conductor of electricity or as a non-conductor (insulator).

Shellac   Refined lac, a yellowish gum, or resin, produced by the lac insect of India and Burma.

Silicon chip   A microelectronic circuit incorporated into a single tiny piece of the semiconductor material silicon.

Telegraph   A method of communicating by sending coded electrical signals along a wire.

Telemetry   Using radio or telegraph to transmit the readings of remote measuring instruments.

Telephone   An electrical device for transmitting speech along a wire.

Teletex   A form of telegraph used for sending text from one word processor to another.

Teletext   Computer information compiled by broadcasting companies and broadcast alongside normal television programmes. It can be received by anyone with the right type of television set.

Television   A system for sending and receiving pictures using radio waves.

Telex   A form of telegraph used for sending and receiving text. Letters typed by the sender are automatically encoded and transmitted by the sender's machine. On arrival at the receiver's machine, they are decoded and printed out.

Thermionic valve   A system of electrodes (metal conductors unattached at one end) in an enclosed glass vessel that contains no air. When the cathode (negative electrode) and anode (positive electrode) are connected correctly into an electrical circuit, the cathode heats up and a stream of electrons passes from it to the anode. See also diode valve and triode valve.

Transistor   An electronic device, made up of three layers of a semiconductor material, that performs the same functions as a triode valve, but is more reliable and consumes less power.

Triode valve A type of thermionic valve that has a third electrode, the grid, in between the cathode and anode. A high negative charge applied to the grid prevents electrons from reaching the anode and the valve can thus be used as a switch. If a small, varying signal is applied to the grid, a large variation is produced in the current flowing from the cathode to the anode. The valve thus amplifies the signal to the grid.

TXE2 Telephone Exchange Electronic No. 2, a type of telephone exchange used in Britain since 1966.

TXE4 Larger capacity version of the TXE2 telephone exchange used in Britain.

Valve See Thermionic valve.

Video disc A laser disc used for reproducing television pictures.

Video recorder A machine that uses magnetic tape to record and play back television pictures.

Videotex Computer information, stored on central database computers, that can be displayed on a television screen. See teletext and viewdata.

Viewdata Computer information compiled by a viewdata service (e.g. Prestel) and transmitted to subscribers via the telephone system.

Word processor A computer or computer program designed specifically for producing text.

Further Reading

Lambert, Mark, and Insley, Jane, **Communications and Transport** (Orbis 1986).

Lines, Cliff, **Exploring Communications** (Wayland 1988).

Mondy, David (Ed.), **The International Encyclopedia of Aviation** (Octopus Books 1977).

Myring, Lynn, and Graham, Ian, **Information Revolution** (Usborne Publishing 1983).

Myring, Lynn, and Kimmitt, Maurice, **Lasers** (Usborne Publishing 1984).

Wheen, Francis, **Television** (Century Publishing 1985).

Picture acknowledgements

The illustrations in this book were supplied by: BBC Hulton 7, 10, 11 (below), 12 (above), 13 (above), 16, 17 (above), 18 (both), 19, 22, 23, 24 (both), 26; British Telecom (TeleFocus) *front cover* (both), *back cover*, 12 (below), 20, 28 (above), 31, 32, 39, 41, 44 (both), 45 (above); the Mansell Collection 9, 17 (below); Francesca Motisi 4 (main); Christine Osborne 32; Ann Ronan 4 (inset), 5 (both), 6 (both), 8, 11 (above), 13 (below); TOPHAM 25 (both), 27, 28 (both), 29, 37 (below), 38, 40, 42 (both), 43; Zefa *title page*, 30, 34, 35, 37 (top), 45 (below). The remaining pictures are from the Wayland Picture Library.

Index